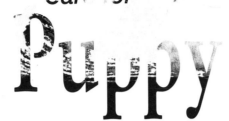

# CONTENTS

22 NOV

First published in 1985 by
William Collins Sons & Co Ltd, London
New edition published in 1990

Reprinted by HarperCollins*Publishers* 1992, 1994 (twice), 1995, 1996,
1997 (twice)

This is a fully revised and extended edition of *Care for your Puppy*, first
published in 1985 and reprinted 5 times

© Royal Society for the Prevention of Cruelty to Animals 1985, 1990

Text of the 1985 edition by Tina Hearne; text revisions and additions for
this edition by Michael Pollard

Designed and edited by The Templar Company plc
Pippbrook Mill, London Road, Dorking, Surrey RH4 1JE

Front cover photograph: Animal Ark, London
Text photographs: Animal Photography Ltd, Bruce Coleman Ltd,
Solitaire *(also back cover, top)*, Tony Stone Worldwide, Sue Streeter
*(also back cover, centre)*

Illustrations: Terry Riley/David Lewis Artists and
Robert Morton/Bernard Thornton Artists

**A catalogue record for this book is available
from the British Library**

ISBN 0 00 412541 X

Printed in Hong Kong by Sing Cheong Printing Co. Ltd.

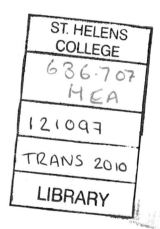

First things first, animals are fun. Anybody who has ever enjoyed the company of a pet knows well enough just how strong the bond between human and animal can be. Elderly or lonely people often depend on a pet for their only company, and this can be a rewarding relationship for both human and animal. Doctors have proved that animals can be instrumental in the prevention of and recovery from mental or physical disease. Children learn the meaning of loyalty, unselfishness and friendship by growing up with animals.

But the commitment to an animal doesn't begin and end with a visit to the local pet shop. A pet should never be given as a 'surprise' present. The decision to bring a pet into your home should always be discussed and agreed by all the members of your family. Bear in mind that parents are ultimately responsible for the health and well-being of the animal for the whole of its lifetime. If you are not prepared for the inevitable expense, time, patience and occasional frustration involved, then the RSPCA would much rather that you didn't have a pet.

Armed with the facts, aware of the pitfalls but still confident of your ability to give a pet a good home, the next step is to find where you can get an animal from. Seek the advice of a veterinary surgeon or RSPCA Inspector about reputable local breeders or suppliers. Do consider the possibility of offering a home to an animal from an RSPCA establishment. There are no animals more deserving of loving owners.

As for the care of your pet, you should find in this book all you need to know to keep it happy, healthy and rewarding for many years to come. Responsible ownership means happy pets. Enjoy the experience!

*Terence C. Bate*

TERENCE BATE BVSc, LLB, MRCVS
*Chief Veterinary Officer, RSPCA*

# Introduction

Before you commit yourself to a puppy, think carefully about whether you can afford to keep a dog, whether your home is suitable, and whether dog ownership will fit into your lifestyle.

- **Keeping a dog is quite costly**. Apart from the obvious initial expenses such as the purchase price and cost of housing and accessories, there is the mounting cost of feeding as the puppy grows bigger. Insurance can help cover the cost of the veterinary care which is sure to be needed from time to time, but even vaccinations can be expensive. You must also be prepared for the cost of boarding kennels when you go on holiday.
- **Dogs need space**. When you are considering whether your house and garden are large enough, remember that many small puppies grow into larger dogs. Sadly, many of the larger breeds are abandoned or have to be rehomed when the owners discover that their homes are too small. Make sure you know what size your puppy will grow to, how much space it will need and how much it will eat.
- **Dogs need company**. They are pack animals by instinct and are unhappy if they are left too much on their own. You should not take on the commitment of a puppy unless someone will be at home most of the time. You must also be prepared to devote some of your time each day to exercise, training and grooming. Your puppy will grow up to regard you, its owner, as its pack leader and will expect to take part in the life of your family.
- If you are excessively house-proud, you may not be prepared to tolerate the inevitable stains and smells associated with a small puppy, possible damage to furniture and furnishings and unavoidable dog hairs.
- Many young puppies suffer stress as a result of the arrival of a new spouse or a new baby, or removal to another new home. It is best to delay buying a puppy until you can offer it stability during the first few months of its life.

Cross-breds or mongrels? These eight-week old puppies suggest possible Alsatian and Labrador ancestry.

Among pedigree dogs, the Cocker Spaniel is a popular choice. It is a good companion, but can be difficult with young children. Its appetite for exercise is enormous.

# Pedigree or mongrel?

A large proportion of puppies are born as a result of accidental or casually arranged matings. Puppies of unplanned pregnancies are usually cross-breds or mongrels and tend, for genetic reasons, to be physically more robust and temperamentally more stable than some inbred pedigree puppies.

## PEDIGREE PUPPIES

Pedigree puppies have parents of the same recognized breed. They are certainly the most expensive, but may not necessarily be the 'best buy'. Many puppies suffer from over-breeding, resulting in genetic weaknesses and sometimes difficulties of temperament. Against this, most breeds have largely consistent patterns of behaviour so that the owner knows what to expect of the grown dog. Pedigree puppies should be bought from a recognized breeder.

## CROSS-BRED PUPPIES

Cross-breds are the puppies born to pure-bred parents of different breeds. The puppies will inherit half their genes from the dam, half from the sire. As the genes control all the myriad characteristics of size, shape, colour, coat type, and so on, as well as intelligence and temperamental traits, the resulting puppies will show a combination of both parents' looks and temperaments, and can be highly attractive.

## MONGREL PUPPIES

Mongrel puppies are those of mixed ancestry and no definable breed. When breeding pedigree puppies the choice of parents (and therefore of genetic material) is strictly limited; with the mongrel population the choice is unlimited. This accounts for the diversity, strength and hardiness of mongrel puppies, and for their relative lack of inherited and congenital disorders. They can make delightful pets.

The RSPCA and other animal welfare organizations are good sources of healthy mongrels.

# *Which sex?*

Personal taste apart, there is very little significance in the choice between a male and a female puppy. Traditionally, bitches are thought to be more home-loving and dogs more aggressive, but if, as recommended, the puppies are neutered these distinctions largely disappear.

## FEMALES

Most female puppies can be expected to reach puberty at about eight months, when they will normally have their first oestrus or season ('come on heat'). For the rest of their life they will then season every six months, each lasting for about three weeks, during which males over a wide area are attracted by scent. In the first few days of the season there are discharges of mucus and blood which can stain furniture and carpets. Bitches in season constantly clean themselves and may show changes in temperament such as unnatural lethargy or excitability.

For these reasons, but mostly because of the high risk of pregnancy, most owners seek to control oestrus. Some pen up the bitch, or board her at kennels; some attempt control by deodorant sprays; some use prescribed hormonal treatment. The most satisfactory means of control, from the point of view of both the bitch and its owner, is spaying (see opposite).

## MALES

A male puppy can be expected to reach maturity at between eight and twelve months, by which time he will be displaying characteristic dog behaviour. This may include roaming in search of bitches, and aggression with other dogs or with people. He will also spray urine to mark territory. Such behaviour can be worrying, dangerous and embarrassing. Unlike the female, the male is sexually active throughout the year.

The male's sexual behaviour can be controlled medicinally, but many owners prefer to have the dog castrated by a veterinary surgeon.

At nine days old, these puppies already have pigment freckles on their noses.

# Neutering

The abandonment of thousands of unwanted puppies each year is one of the tragedies of modern society. Unless it is intended to breed seriously from a puppy and the owner can guarantee good homes for the offspring, or unless there are veterinary reasons, a pet dog should be neutered.

## WHAT AGE TO NEUTER?

Veterinary surgeons have differing views on the best age for neutering but, bearing in mind that some bitches reach puberty at six months and some dogs at eight, new owners of puppies should not delay long before taking veterinary advice. Generally, bitches should be spayed before the first season, to avoid any risk of pregnancy, and dogs between seven and twelve months.

Both spaying and castration are carried out under general anaesthetic. The operations are simple, complications are rare and recovery is swift. Certainly the risks to a bitch are less than the risks of pregnancy and birth.

Exploration and play are the mainsprings of puppies' lives. These are between eleven and twelve weeks old.

## ADVANTAGES OF NEUTERING

Unneutered males will be attracted by bitches on heat in the locality, and will follow them if they get the chance. This can lead to dog-fights, traffic accidents, the worrying of farm livestock or, at best, worry for the owner when the dog goes missing. If unable to mate, dogs may simulate intercourse with a chair or a visitor's leg. Unneutered bitches on heat will attract attention from dogs and must, in effect, be confined under close house arrest. They are also prone to phantom pregnancies which will need veterinary treatment. Sexual frustration frequently results in over-excitement in bitches and aggression in dogs.

It is a common belief that neutering leads to overweight. This is untrue, but a neutered animal may well need less food than before. Veterinary advice should be taken. As neutering is normally done at the time of change from puppy rations to an adult diet (see pp. 20-3) it is not difficult to make appropriate adjustments.

# Size

Dogs vary in size more than any other pet animal. In height they range from the Irish Wolfhound, standing 81 cm/32 in at the shoulder, down to the Yorkshire Terrier, standing only 20 cm/8 in.

The weight range is just as great. The Chihuahua weighs perhaps 1 kg/2 lb, the St Bernard 70 kg/150 lb, and mongrels can be as much as 36 kg/80 lb. Size, then, is an important consideration all too often ignored when choos-

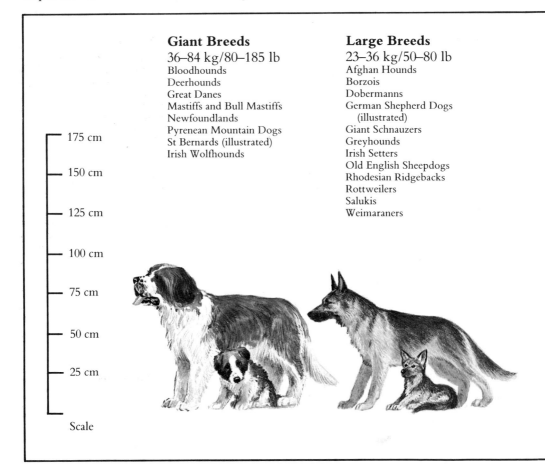

**Giant Breeds**
36–84 kg/80–185 lb
Bloodhounds
Deerhounds
Great Danes
Mastiffs and Bull Mastiffs
Newfoundlands
Pyrenean Mountain Dogs
St Bernards (illustrated)
Irish Wolfhounds

**Large Breeds**
23–36 kg/50–80 lb
Afghan Hounds
Borzois
Dobermanns
German Shepherd Dogs
  (illustrated)
Giant Schnauzers
Greyhounds
Irish Setters
Old English Sheepdogs
Rhodesian Ridgebacks
Rottweilers
Salukis
Weimaraners

175 cm

150 cm

125 cm

100 cm

75 cm

50 cm

25 cm

Scale

ing a dog. For some reason people will not accept how much small puppies can grow.

For ordinary family life, dogs from the small and middle ranges do best. Most are physically robust, and fit with reasonable comfort into a family-sized house and car, enabling them to accompany their owners on most outings.

As a general rule, the large breeds are remarkably tolerant of children and good guard dogs too, but they do need much more space.

The size of a breed is not necessarily a good guide to its lifestyle. For example, all spaniels are essentially outdoor dogs and need a good deal of daily exercise. The Dalmatian, although classed as a medium breed like the Spaniels, needs rather less exercise but will often find itself family duties such as guarding children. It is important to choose a puppy whose lifestyle, as an adult, will match your own.

### Medium Breeds
13.5–23 kg/30–50 lb
Basset Hounds
Boxers
Bulldogs
Chow Chows
Collies, Bearded Collies, and
    Border Collies
Dalmatians
Keeshonds
Pointers and German Pointers
Poodles (Standard), (illustrated)
Retrievers (including Labradors)
Samoyeds
Spaniels (Clumber, Field, English
    and Welsh Springer, Sussex,
    Irish Water)
Terriers (Airedale, Irish, Kerry
    Blue, Soft-Coated Wheaten)

### Small Breeds
4.5–13.5 kg/10–30 lb
Basenjis
Beagles
Bull Terriers, and Staffordshire
    Bull Terriers
Dachshunds
French Bulldogs
Poodles (Miniature)
Schipperkes
Schnauzers and Miniature
    Schnauzers
Shetland Sheepdogs
Shih Tzu
Spaniels (Cocker and American
    Cocker)
Terriers (except those listed as
    medium or toy) (Scottish
    Terrier illustrated)
Welsh Corgis
Whippets

### Toy Breeds
1–4.5 kg/2–10 lb
Cavalier King Charles Spaniels
Chihuahuas (illustrated)
English Toy Terriers
Griffons Bruxsellois
Italian Greyhounds
Japanese Chin
King Charles Spaniels
Maltese
Miniature Pinschers
Papillons
Pekingese
Pomeranians
Pugs
Silky Terriers
Yorkshire Terriers

6 ft

5 ft

4 ft

3 ft

2 ft

1 ft

Scale

# *Breed types*

Not all pedigree puppies will grow into suitable family pets, for each breed was originally evolved to fulfil a purpose for which its inherent qualities of speed, size, stamina, conformation and temperament are well suited.

**Hounds** Hounds were bred to hunt other animals (shown here in brackets) either by sight or by scent. Examples of sight hounds are the Afghan (leopard), Borzoi (wolf), Greyhound (hare and deer), Irish Wolfhound (wolf), Rhodesian Ridgeback (lion) and Saluki (gazelle). All are long-legged and swift.

Afghan Hound

Scent hounds, by contrast, are short-legged and well adapted to follow a trail by scent. They include the Basset Hound, Beagle and Bloodhound. Hounds have both the instinct and stamina to range wide over the countryside.

**Terriers** These are the smallest of the hunting breeds. They take their name from the Latin word *terra*, meaning earth, for they work by going to earth themselves to bolt their quarry. As so many of the breed names suggest – Airedale, Border, Irish, Kerry Blue, Lakeland, Scottish, Skye, Welsh, West Highland etc – they were kept on large estates and farms to control vermin, badgers, foxes and otters. By nature tough, energetic, loyal and fearless, those terriers which adapt to pet life are valued as lively companions and reliable house dogs, but may be aggressive with strangers.

Fox Terrier

**Gundogs** These breeds are trained to assist man in finding, pointing and retrieving game birds and water-fowl, whether from land or from water. Because their traditional role is not to kill but to co-operate, they are obedient and dependable. Gundogs include Setters, Pointers, Retrievers and Spaniels. Of these, the Golden Retriever and Labrador Retriever probably adapt to pet life better than any other sporting breeds, but their superb natures should not be abused by lack of exercise.

American Cocker Spaniel

**Working dogs**   These include the breeds trained to herd sheep and cattle, e.g. the Collie, German Shepherd Dog, Old English Sheepdog and Welsh Corgi; those bred to guard people, property and animals, e.g. the Boxer, Bull Mastiff, Dobermann, Great Dane and Rottweiler; those polar breeds used for drawing sleighs, e.g. the Alaskan Malamute, Samoyed and Siberian Husky; and the two famous rescue breeds, the St Bernard and the Newfoundland. All are country dogs, and must not be kept too confined.

It is important to remember that response to training and the need for very active lives are characteristics in all working breeds. No one should consider the ownership of a working dog unless it can be guaranteed very strict and comprehensive training, including obedience training, plenty of exercise and a lifestyle in which it can use or sublimate its working potential. If not, difficulties and frustration for both owner and dog are inevitable.

**Utility dogs**   Utility dogs are those breeds not included in the sporting or working categories above, yet which were once bred to a particular role, although most are now successfully kept as pets. Notable members of this group are the Bulldog (for bull-baiting), Chow Chow (bred for fur and meat in the East), Dalmatian (carriage escort dog), Keeshond (Dutch barge dog), Poodle (performing dog bred from a water retriever) and Shih Tzu (lion dog of China).

**Toy dogs**   These include miniature versions of the larger breeds and have been bred as lapdogs or for the show bench. They are inexpensive to feed, need little exercise and have many devotees among those who like a constant companion about the house. However, selective breeding for small size has rendered them, as a group, delicate and rather excitable. Well-known toy breeds are the Chihuahua, Maltese, Papillon, Pekingese, Pomeranian, Pug and Yorkshire Terrier.

Not only the toy breeds suffer hereditary defects. Centuries of inbreeding have weakened many breeds, making them prone to such defects as cataracts, deafness, haemophilia, elongated soft palates, epilepsy, hip dysplasia, hernias, progressive retinal atrophy and many more. Early veterinary examination is recommended.

German Shepherd Dog

Shih Tzu

Chihuahua

# Biology

**Stance** The Dalmatian illustrates an example of good stance, but selective breeding has produced many variations, which can predispose to certain disorders.

*The hind limbs* The crouching stance of the German Shepherd Dog is achieved because its hind limbs are in permanent flexion, resulting in a sloping spine and exacerbating the possibility of posterior paralysis and hip dysplasia. In contrast, the overextension of the hind limbs of taller dogs, such as Great Danes and Newfoundlands, can cause the stifle joint to dislocate backwards.

*The fore limbs* The enormous width of the chest of the Bulldog can cause the fore limbs to bow, resulting in uneven wear on the joints. The long-backed, short-legged breeds such as Dachshunds may also have bowed fore limbs and splayed out toes. Both problems can result in arthritis.

**Head and eyes** Selective breeding has resulted in variations ranging from the elongated eyes of the long-nosed dogs such as the Greyhound and Collie to the protuberant eyes of short-faced breeds such as the Pug and Pekingese.

In general, the long-nosed dogs suffer fewer disadvantages than the short-faced breeds. The short-nosed dogs can suffer breathing difficulties, overcrowded teeth, and eczema in the folds of the skin. The protuberant eyes, just by their prominence, are predisposed to irritation and accidental damage that may give rise to corneal ulcers. They also flatten and distort the tear ducts so tears tend to run down the cheeks.

**Genitalia** There is an increasing number of male pedigree puppies whose testicles do not descend into the scrotal sac normally. At the time of purchase, it may be found that the puppy has only one testicle in the scrotum – or even none. This is usually a hereditary defect, and it is reprehensible in law to sell such a puppy without drawing attention to the condition.

The undescended testicle can sometimes be located in the groin. If not, then it is inside the abdominal cavity. Quite often it will descend at a later date, but if after six months this has not occurred, it is not likely to do so. Unfortunately, such a condition can lead to serious problems from middle age onwards.

It is not possible to judge whether the development and function of the female sex organs are satisfactory until the puppy has had her first season (p.6). This is one reason for not spaying too early.

**Claws** A puppy's nails should not be clipped while it is very young. Once allowed out, after vaccination (p.36), the puppy will usually wear down its own claws naturally by exercising on hard ground and pavements. If clipped before this, there is a tendency for the claws to lose their curvature and grow straight.

Split and fractured claws, damaged by the exuberant play of puppies, can cause bleeding and tenderness, and sometimes infection of the nail-bed, all of which need veterinary attention.

**Dew claws** Puppies are born with dew claws on the fore limbs, and 20–30 per cent also have dew claws on the hind limbs. The front ones seldom give trouble, but the hind ones tend to get torn and may bleed profusely.

Although any mutilation is questionable on ethical grounds, many veterinary surgeons feel that, to avoid trauma, it is preferable to remove the hind dew claws at the age of 3–5 days. There are certain exceptions. For instance, the breed standard for Pyrenean Mountain Dogs requires that the hind dew claws should be retained.

Short-faced Pekingese

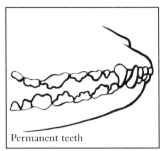

Permanent teeth

**Teething** Some puppies have trouble teething. They may have a gum infection or, more often, sore gums and persistent milk teeth. Gum infections will need veterinary treatment, but chewing on a large marrow bone, or a manufactured dog chew, will help to relieve soreness and complete shedding of the milk teeth.

If the deciduous canines are not shed in time, it may be necessary to have them extracted. If not, they can either cause the permanent canines to be displaced,

**Dalmatian**

or cause them to decay as a result of food being trapped between the persistent milk canines and the newly erupting permanent teeth.

**Milk teeth** Most puppies are born toothless, although the outline of the teeth can be seen in the gums. By the time the puppy is eight weeks, it will have a full set of deciduous or milk teeth. Indeed, many puppies will have cut them all by the age of four weeks.

A full set of milk teeth comprises 3 incisors at the front, then 1 canine, and 3 premolars at the back on each side of the upper jaw, and the same for the lower jaw. This gives a total of 28 teeth.

The third premolars and canines erupt before the incisors, which are cut in succession (from the sides towards the centre of the mouth), and those in the upper jaw appear before those in the lower jaw. The first and second premolars are the last to erupt. Puppies lose their deciduous teeth between two and four months.

**Permanent teeth** A full set of permanent teeth comprises, in the upper jaw, 3 incisors at the front, then 1 canine, 4 premolars and 2 molars on each side and in the lower jaw, 3 incisors, 1 canine, 4 premolars, and 3 molars on each side. This gives a total of 42 teeth.

There is considerable variation, but in general big dogs teethe before the toy breeds. Between two and five months of age, the permanent upper front incisors erupt, then the lower incisors, followed by the premolars. The canines are usually through by the age of six months. Last to appear are the permanent molars, but even these are in place and dentition is complete by the age of eight months.

**Tail docking** Traditionally, certain breeds of dogs – for example, the Pembroke Welsh Corgi and the Old English Sheepdog – have had their tails docked. The purpose of this has been largely cosmetic. Tail-docking has become an increasingly contentious issue in recent years, and it is banned in many countries. In Britain, the RSPCA has campaigned against the practice for many years.

Scottie with erect ears

**Ears** A puppy with erect ears is less likely to suffer ear trouble than a puppy with folded ears. Folded ears prevent good ventilation of the ear canal not only by obstructing its entrance, but also by distorting the canal further by their sheer weight.

Debris such as dust, grit, grass seeds and wax accumulates and is trapped in a folded ear, predisposing to infections caused by anaerobic bacteria which thrive in such an environment.

Woolly-coated dogs such as Poodles, which do not moult, need to have the hair in the ear canal plucked to increase the circulation of air and to prevent the accumulation of debris.

Ear cropping is one mutilation that is thankfully not carried out in the UK, but in certain European countries, for example, some breeds may still have their ears cropped (i.e. cut) to 'improve' their outline.

# Housing

## THE NEED FOR PRIVACY

Every puppy should be allocated a place of its own where it can be territorial and have some privacy away from the family. Fortunate puppies will have one place in the house and a kennel or outhouse in the garden.

If a puppy is to grow up with a happy lack of neurotic behaviour traits such as chewing its own paws, and howling and barking when alone, this privacy is of paramount importance. No puppy should be left alone all day while the family is out, but quiet periods alone are beneficial. The family must accept this fact, and avoid disturbing and over-stimulating the puppy just because it is new and appealing.

In the house it is difficult to find a place that is exclusively the puppy's domain, but the puppy bed must be put in a relatively undisturbed place, free of draughts but also away from any direct source of heat. Sometimes a conservatory is suitable, but beware of overheating in summer when a glazed roof can concentrate the heat of the sun.

## THE PUPPY'S BED

In the early days it is necessary to ensure that the puppy actually sleeps in its bed. Certainly for the first few nights a new puppy will be likely to try to stop you from leaving it alone. Resist the temptation to allow the puppy into your own room: it is bad training for the puppy and there is always the risk that fleas (which your puppy may have) will breed in your bedding (p.38).

A very suitable puppy bed is illustrated. Made of rigid plastic, it is available in a range of sizes and is relatively inexpensive, light, washable, waterproof, and reasonably resistant to the puppy's destructive skills. It is meant to be used with soft, disposable or washable bedding.

The traditional dog basket made of woven willow is not suitable for most puppies which would simply unravel it. Neither are 'bean bag' beds or foam bags suitable. Most young puppies would chew these and would risk swallowing pieces of the filling.

**Playpen** Many owners find it very convenient to use a playpen to contain a young puppy at night and for periods during the day. A child's playpen can be adapted with the addition of wire-mesh or weld mesh, and for as long as it contains the puppy safely, the playpen can be used outdoors or in the house.

**Flooring** Until the puppy has learnt bladder control, its playpen will obviously have to stand on a washable floor when in the house. It is very important to clean the floor thoroughly when mopping up after accidents, in order to remove the puppy's own odour from the spot. If this is not done, the puppy will continue to urinate and defecate in the same place.

Use newspapers on the floor to help in the house-training of small puppies (p.28).

**Playthings** The puppy derives great pleasure from a big marrow bone, but only offer a raw beef shin bone. It is a natural plaything, cleans the teeth, helps in the shedding of the milk teeth, exercises the jaws and provides some calcium. Never give a puppy small bones that may break or splinter, and also beware of a puppy swallowing excessive amounts of powder-fine but indissoluble fragments from cooked bones. Dog chews are a good substitute and certainly less hazardous. As such, many veterinary surgeons recommend that these be given to puppies in preference to bones.

There is a wide variety of puppy toys available. Choose with care and avoid those which mimic personal possessions – such as slippers – too closely, or it will hardly be surprising if the puppy makes the mistake of thinking all slippers are playthings.

## AN OUTDOOR KENNEL

As household pets, most dogs are given a base in the home and take part in the life of the family. There may, however, be practical reasons why this is not possible, especially with some of the larger, heavier-coated breeds. Dogs are quite adaptable to life in a dry, well-insulated kennel, and will if necessary grow a suitably thick, protective winter coat.

A puppy which it is planned to house outside should be bought in spring or summer so that it has time to acclimatize as winter approaches. A dog kept outside will still identify with the family as its pack, and special care should be taken to give it plenty of human contact.

## KENNEL DESIGN

When choosing or designing a kennel, the three vital requirements are that it should be weatherproof, draughtproof and well-ventilated. It should be raised about 10 cm/ 4 in off the ground to allow for ventilation underneath and to avoid damp penetration. The roof should be pitched to shed rain and snow, and the eaves should overhang sufficiently to carry water away from the walls. As a protection against draughts, there should be a porch and the entrance should be at the front rather than at a gable end. The front (or alternatively the roof) should be hinged so that the kennel can be opened up for easy cleaning.

The eventual adult size of the dog should be borne in mind; a growing puppy will not mind having extra space, provided that its bed is snug, but an adult dog will be very unhappy in a kennel that is too small. As a general guide, the kennel should be big enough to allow the adult dog freedom of movement, and the door should be at least 1½ times the width of the adult.

Essential kennel furniture consists of a good bed and warm bedding.

## SITING

Careful consideration should be given to the siting of the kennel. It should be placed so that the door is away from prevailing wind and out of the heat of the midday sun. If possible, the site should allow the puppy to see the most frequently used house door and some of the activity around. The fact that a puppy is kept outside and therefore has more freedom than one kept in the house should not be made an excuse to deny it accompanied exercise or the love and attention that every dog expects and is entitled to.

# *Choosing a puppy*

With these three Yorkshire Terrier pups, as with all pedigree dogs, an official pedigree certificate should be supplied by the vendor, and the purchase should be conditional upon veterinary clearance.

The most important thing about selecting a puppy is to take plenty of time over it. Impulse purchases, of puppies as of other things, are often regretted.

## WHERE TO BUY

Your local veterinary surgeon can advise you on reputable local breeders and other sources of supply. Alternatively, animal welfare organizations can often help. Many breed societies have 'rescue' associations offering puppies which have been abandoned or are not required for breeding purposes. Some of the latter may have minor defects of appearance which make them unsuitable for showing or breeding but do not affect their suitability as pets. An alternative source is a reputable animal home. Puppies should not be obtained from pet shops or street markets.

Whenever possible, see the puppy with its mother and siblings. Look for an active, healthy puppy (see p.35) and do not be tempted to choose the runt of the litter out of pity.

## DOCUMENTATION

Puppies should preferably have received the first vaccinations in their immunization programme before they leave the dam, and the vendor should supply an interim vaccination certificate. Purchase must be after, or conditional on, a satisfactory veterinary examination. Pedigree puppies should be accompanied by an official pedigree certificate. The other essential piece of documentation for the new owner is a diet sheet showing how the puppy has been fed so far. Moving to a new home is enough of an upset for a young puppy without adding to it by the stress of unfamiliar food. Any desired changes from the former diet should be made gradually once the puppy has settled in.

In law, buying a puppy attracts the same statutory rights as any other purchase. Many good breeders also ask that if, at any time in the future, the dog cannot be kept, it should be returned to them.

# Introducing the new puppy

The change from the familiar comfort of its dam and siblings to the novel surroundings of a new home is bewildering and potentially frightening for a puppy, and every effort must be made to calm its fears and provide an orderly introduction to its new way of life. Such questions as where the puppy's bed is to go, where its food and water bowls will be sited, and which parts of the house it is allowed access to, should have been decided in advance. The bed and bowls should already be in place, so that from the start the puppy can see that its essential needs have been provided for.

## CHILDREN AND PETS

It is difficult to restrain young children from gathering round to admire the new puppy, but for the first day or two they should keep their distance and avoid noise and sudden movements. When the puppy feels sufficiently at ease in its new surroundings it will come forward of its own accord and indicate that it is ready to make friends. Very young children should not be left unsupervised with a puppy.

The puppy's name should be used frequently from the beginning. After the settling-in period, the puppy will be ready to start playing, but games must be gentle and should

In its new home, a puppy's instinct may be to run for cover. A quiet, calm approach will enable the newcomer to settle in more quickly.

not go on for more than a few minutes at a session.

If there are any other pets in the house, these must be introduced to the new arrival with care. Cats tend to treat new puppies with caution, and may keep well out of their way for a few days while they assess the risks. Care should be taken that, in the excitement of the new arrival, older pets continue to receive their share of attention.

Cats will usually stand their ground even when faced by a large inquisitive puppy. Indeed, size is no barrier to friendship and cats are often more tolerant of large dogs than small ones.

## TEMPORARY ISOLATION

Until the first course of vaccinations has been completed, usually at about ten to fourteen weeks, your puppy must not be allowed into areas where other, unvaccinated, dogs may have walked. This means that the puppy must be confined to your own yard or garden, and must be carried if it ventures outside (for example, to visit the veterinary surgery).

# Feeding

## THE BALANCED DIET

The constituents of a balanced diet are protein, fat, carbo-hydrate, vitamins, minerals, water and roughage.

**Protein** (meat, offal, fish, and occasionally cheese and eggs) must account for a considerable proportion of the diet. Meat and fish fit for human consumption may be fed raw; offals should be cooked and fed only in moderation.

**Carbohydrate** is obtained from such cereal foods as biscuit and biscuit meal, wholemeal bread and, for young puppies, puppy meal, cooked rice, baby cereals and porridge.

**Fat** is obtained from the protein foods and from milk.

**Extra vitamins and minerals** should be given to puppies in a calcium-rich mineral/vitamin supplement.

**Roughage** is provided by cereal foods and vegetables. As dogs synthesize vitamin C, greens need not be given.

**Fresh drinking water** must always be within reach.

**Convenience foods** If tinned meat is to be given, it is recommended that it be introduced into the diet progress-ively from the age of about four months. Some varieties contain a mixture of proteins and carbohydrates with sup-plements, and these brands are designed to meet all the nutritional needs. Others contain meat intended to be fed with cereal such as biscuit or biscuit meal. When additional cereal is indicated, feed an equal volume of cereal and tinned food.

Dried foods are also intended to provide for all the nutritional needs. However, they have the disadvantage of monotony and may create increased thirst in the puppy which must be satisfied by the provision of a generous supply of fresh drinking water. Some dried foods require the addition of water and a period of soaking before they are put down.

In all cases follow the manufacturer's advice about quan-tities, always allowing for individual variation between puppies.

Veterinary surgeons are always glad to advise on feeding if any difficulties arise.

## Guide to the daily feeding of puppies  *(allow for individual variation)*

| Type of breed & ADULT weight | Age (months) | Meat (weight when raw) | Milk (maximum quantity) |
|---|---|---|---|
| **Toy:** up to 4.5 kg (10 lb) | 2–4<br>4–6<br>6–9 | 30–60 g (1–2 oz)<br>60–85 g (2–3 oz)<br>85–110 g (3–4 oz) | 70 ml (⅛ pt)<br>110 ml (⅕ pt)<br>140 ml (¼ pt) |
| **Small:** 4.5–13.5 kg (10–30 lb) | 2–4<br>4–6<br>6–9 | 60–110 g (2–4 oz)<br>110–170 g (4–6 oz)<br>170–225 g (6–8 oz) | 140 ml (¼ pt)<br>140 ml (¼ pt)<br>140 ml (¼ pt) |
| **Medium:** 13.5–23 kg (30–50 lb) | 2–4<br>4–6<br>6–9 | 85–170 g (3–6 oz)<br>170–250 g (6–9 oz)<br>250–335 g (9–12 oz) | 280 ml (½ pt)<br>280 ml (½ pt)<br>280 ml (½ pt) |
| **Large:** 23–36 kg (50–80 lb) | 2–4<br>4–6<br>6–9 | 110–225 g (4–8 oz)<br>225–390 g (8–14 oz)<br>390–560 g (14–20 oz) | 425 ml (¾ pt)<br>570 ml (1 pt)<br>570 ml (1 pt) |
| **Giant:** over 36 kg (80 lb) | 2–4<br>4–6<br>6–9 | 170–335 g (6–12 oz)<br>335–560 g (12–20 oz)<br>560 g+   (20 oz +) | 570 ml (1 pt)<br>855 ml (1½ pt)<br>855 ml (1½ pt) |

Add an equal *weight* of biscuit meal or other suitable cereal to meat (weighed when raw)

**Milk**  This should be considered as a food rather than as a drink. By the age of six months, when milk and cereal meals are discontinued, milk should be offered separately. Avoid giving a puppy very cold milk taken straight from a refrigerator.

### THE PUPPY AT TWO–FOUR MONTHS

Whenever possible, follow the breeder's feeding notes while the eight-week-old puppy is settling in to its new home, and make changes only gradually. Such very young puppies need food that is easy to digest, and so minced meat (particularly white meat), flaked fish, cooked cereal foods (see above) and milk are important constituents of the diet. At this age the puppy will need four regular meals a day: milk and cereal at 8 a.m; meat and cereal at noon; milk and cereal at 4 p.m.; and meat and cereal at 8 p.m. Avoid feeding milk and meat together.

### THE PUPPY AT FOUR–TEN MONTHS

As the puppy grows, the number of meals given is reduced, while the amount of food offered at each is increased. At four months omit one of the milk and cereal meals; at six months omit the other. At this time begin to offer a dish of milk separately. By ten months, only small breeds will need two meals a day. Larger breeds will thrive on one main meal and one much smaller meal.

### VEGETARIAN FOODS

Vegetarians and vegans sometimes wish to provide their dogs with a non-meat diet. Such foods are available, but they should be used only with veterinary advice. (Note: a cat's diet, however, *must* include protein of animal origin.)

### TREATS

Most puppies will try to beg titbits from the family, but however difficult they are to resist the sensible owner will take a firm line from the beginning. It is always difficult to

restrain children from sharing their sweets and crisps with the family pet, but these are highly unsuitable foods, especially for puppies. There must be an absolute embargo on children feeding treats to the dog. Puppies can be discouraged by putting a protective hand over the desired item and saying firmly 'Mine!' But it is best to keep temptation out of the way by not eating treats in front of a puppy.

Similarly, from the beginning puppies should be discouraged from begging at family mealtimes. It may be that there are small 'left-overs' which can be given as a treat, but this should take place after the family meal is over and should be fed in the dog's own bowl. However, this should be a special concession rather than a regular occurrence.

Titbits are invaluable in training, and a reward is sometimes appropriate at other times. Suitable items can be obtained at pet shops, though with care — some things sold as 'dog treats' can be equally unsuitable.

If in doubt about feeding bones to puppies, fibre or hide chews make a good substitute and provide excellent exercise for teeth and gums.

Irish Wolfhound bitch and puppies

Maltese bitch and puppies

Golden Retrievers

Basset Hounds

German Shepherd Dog

rriers

Pembroke Corgis

# *Exercise*

Young puppies expend enormous amounts of energy in play, and between their periods of frantic activity should be left to sleep a great deal, undisturbed by children or the household routine.

Their only outdoor playground during the first few months of life is the garden, which must surely be a source of great pleasure to them after the restrictions imposed on them in the house. It may be near impossible to make a garden puppy-proof, but part of it must be enclosed if the puppy is to enjoy some play in the fresh air.

During these early months puppies need to be kept away from other dogs, and even away from places where other dogs may have been, in order to minimize the risk of their contracting disease by cross-infection before their own vaccination regime (p.36) has had time to give them immunity. This need for caution means that going out for even short walks is impossible before the puppy is at least fourteen weeks old.

## COLLARS AND LEADS
As the puppy matures, it will need to be accustomed to wearing a collar and being held on a lead. Try putting the collar on the puppy for short periods – perhaps before feeding, so that the pleasure of the meal will overcome the aversion to wearing a collar – until it is accepted without fuss. Next introduce the puppy to the lead; fix it on to the collar for short periods until the puppy becomes used to that too. Only then can you attempt to take the puppy out in order to encourage it to walk on a lead, but it is unlikely to be ready for any training on the lead until it is nearly six months old (pp. 28–9).

Short-nosed puppies such as Pekingese and Pugs will be safer and more comfortable in a harness. Long-necked breeds will be more comfortable in a broad collar. Avoid using chain collars on long-haired breeds which are better suited to rolled collars. Collars should be loose enough to allow two fingers to slip between the collar and the neck.

Test the fit of the collar frequently. It should be possible to slip two fingers beneath it. New collars will need to be provided as a puppy grows bigger and stronger.

It soon becomes obvious just how much exercise is needed by the big, boisterous breeds such as the Irish Setter, and by the strong, steady breeds such as the Labrador. Increase the exercise programme gradually until, at maturity, the most energetic dogs are having perhaps 16 km/10 miles a day, as well as plenty of freedom in an enclosed garden. A distance of 1.5 km/1 mile is likely to be enough for the smallest breeds.

A safely enclosed garden allows a puppy to enjoy some play in the fresh air

# Basic training

## HOUSE-TRAINING

This should begin in a quiet, unemphatic way as soon as the puppy is brought home. Puppies urinate frequently, and success in house-training depends on anticipating their needs. Regardless of weather, the puppy must be taken outside for a few moments every time on waking, after eating or drinking, etc. Praise or scold gently according to performance. This method is suitable for older and/or larger breeds of puppy.

Small breeds and very young puppies may be paper-trained to urinate and defecate on newspapers spread on the floor. Praise when the papers are used; scold when they are ignored. Gradually move the papers nearer to an outside door and then into the garden before discarding them altogether. Some puppies are house-trained quickly; others take three months to learn bladder control.

**Simple commands**
1. Heel    2. Sit
3. Stay    4. Come

1    2

## SIMPLE COMMANDS

From the age of six months, certain commands can be taught, such as heel, sit, stay and come. The same word must be used invariably, and it must sound distinct from all the others.

It is important to be consistent in the teaching, to teach only one command at a time, and not to overestimate the puppy's span of concentration. Initially, one person should undertake training so that the puppy is not confused. Later, when it is familiar with the commands, it will respond to them when given by others.

Training is achieved by the use of reward and punishment, in the form of praise and scolding. Generous praise should be given for every success, even a belated one.

Scolding is effective only when instant. It is better to ignore a misdemeanour than to confuse the puppy by scolding later when it is behaving well.

Training sessions must be very short to begin with, and the puppy must wear a collar and lead so that the handler has control.

From the age of six months, elementary obedience-training classes are recommended. Although elaborate training is inappropriate for pet dogs, a sensible measure of control is vital for safety and enjoyable companionship.

Most puppies are highly receptive to training and eager to please. However, it is of fundamental importance, when training a puppy, to recognize that the dog is by nature a pack animal and will give its allegiance to the pack leader. In domesticity the owner must assume this role, especially with puppies of the more assertive breeds, or, with minimal opposition, they will assume it for themselves and attempt to dominate the entire household. Calm, firm, consistent and reassuring handling will soon earn their respect.

# Household dangers

Puppies want to investigate the world they find themselves in. This cannot and should not be discouraged, but it can lead puppies into danger. Before a new puppy is brought home, it is worth considering what hazards it will face around the house, and what precautions may be taken. Such ordinary household items as pans of boiling water or hot fat, live cables, toxic cleaners such as bleach, tablets and so on, are potential death-traps and, as such, must be kept well out of reach.

A particular danger area is the garden, so before your puppy is allowed to run free outside, you should check the garden for possible hazards and either remove them or put them behind secure fencing.

**Gates** must close securely and should be so constructed that a puppy cannot wriggle through them. Plastic garden fencing stapled to the gate framework makes a good barrier which can be removed when the puppy is too large to clamber through. Make sure that children understand the importance of closing the gate at all times, and urge this on regular visitors. One danger can be avoided by fixing a postbox to the gate.

Check **fences and hedges** to see that they are puppy-proof. Remember that some breeds, especially terriers, are instinctive diggers and it is possible for a puppy to dig its way out. Plastic garden fencing can be used to block up gaps, fixing it in place with garden canes. Sinking it about 15 cm/6 in into the ground will discourage burrowing. Alternatively, bricks or blocks may be placed against it.

Remove any **ladders** or other fixtures which give access to flat roofs or balconies.

Never move your **car** until you know that the puppy is safely out of the way. Puppies are sometimes excited by car movements, and it is best to restrain them or put them indoors. Always check, before shutting the **garage**, that the puppy is not inside.

The **electric flexes** of garden equipment look like tempt-
ing playthings to a puppy. Confine your dog to a run or to
the house while garden equipment is in use. This also
applies to **mowers, hedge-trimmers** and similar items.

Ensure that **pesticides** and other **garden chemicals** are
stored out of reach, and that they are kept out of the
puppy's way when in use. Before using such products,
check that they are safe for animals; if in doubt, ask your
veterinary surgeon.

**Garden ponds** should be temporarily fenced off while the
puppy is young.

# Grooming

Grooming is always necessary, and not just for good looks. It removes debris such as dust, dead skin, loose hairs and burrs; prevents serious tangling and matting; massages the skin and improves muscle tone; reveals parasites and other problems; and almost certainly gives the puppy a sense of wellbeing.

The amount of grooming needed by a particular puppy will depend on its coat type, but some daily attention should be given to all puppies to accustom them to being handled and examined. Those puppies which will need extensive grooming throughout life must learn to accept it as part of their daily routine.

Dandy brush

### LONG-HAIRED PUPPIES
Many people find long-haired puppies particularly attractive. There are many mongrels and cross-breds with long coats, as well as pedigree puppies such as the Chow Chow, Rough Collie, Setters, Maltese, Old English Sheepdog, Pekingese, Pomeranian, Golden Retriever, Shetland Sheepdog, Shih Tzu and Yorkshire Terrier.

**Brushing, combing and stripping**  If a long coat is to be kept in top condition, it is obligatory to brush and comb it daily to remove the loose hair. Another advantage of daily grooming is that carpets and household furnishings are kept relatively free of puppy hair. Unless preparing for the show bench (when special grooming techniques may be used), brush and comb in the direction the fur grows, and pay particular attention to the feathering on limbs and tail.

Grooming mitt

In more natural conditions, the coat thickens up for the winter and moults for the summer. One major factor nowadays is that in centrally heated houses most puppies are kept too warm and as a result moult throughout the year. The use of a saw-toothed stripping comb will help remove loose hairs, and stripping is particularly desirable in summer when heavy-coated breeds may suffer from excessive heat.

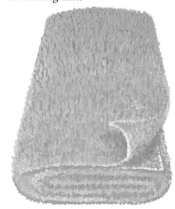

Towel

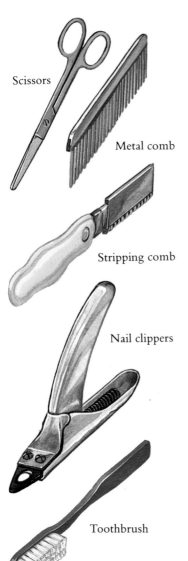

Scissors

Metal comb

Stripping comb

Nail clippers

Toothbrush

## SHORT- AND WIRE-HAIRED BREEDS

Short-haired breeds such as the Boxer, Dalmatian, Greyhound, Pug and Whippet may be brushed or groomed with a rough mitt. The wire-haired terrier breeds, including the Airedale, Fox, Scottish, Sealyham and West Highland White, need grooming with a very stiff brush and metal comb. Daily grooming is desirable, even if brief. Many terriers also benefit from being stripped in summer.

## BATHING

Bathing is not usually recommended for puppies under six months of age. If necessary, in unusual circumstances, use a proprietary shampoo and rinse off each application thoroughly. Towel dry and finish drying with a hairdryer.

## ORAL HYGIENE

All puppies benefit from being accustomed to having their teeth cleaned with a toothbrush and water from an early age. Regular cleaning helps prevent the build-up of plaque and, when they are a little older, tartar. If tartar deposits accumulate, the result will be receding gums, loosened teeth and very bad breath. Puppies most at risk are those of the short-faced and toy breeds which inevitably have overcrowded teeth.

## CLIPPING AND TRIMMING

Puppies such as Poodles and some terrier breeds which need clipping should be taken to a pet beauty parlour for professional attention, at least in the early months. Some owners will become adept at giving a simple trim after they have seen it demonstrated a few times.

Owners of long-haired puppies should use scissors to trim hair between the digits to prevent it becoming uncomfortably matted, and around the anus to prevent matting due to dried faeces.

Nail-clipping (p.12) is not advisable for very young puppies, but may become necessary as they mature. A regular walk on roads or pavements helps keep nails in trim.

## INSPECTION

Grooming sessions also provide an opportunity to check the puppy's general condition. See that the ears are clean, with no signs of discharge or debris such as plant burrs. The eyes and nose should be clear and free of discharge. Check the paws for grit or thorns between the pads.

# The healthy puppy

Puppies are generally resilient, happy and inquisitive, displaying the signs of health listed opposite. When they deviate from these, the owner should seek veterinary advice, initially, perhaps, by telephone. Most veterinary surgeons prefer to see prevaccinated puppies outside normal surgery hours, partly to allow time to discuss such matters as feeding and general care, but also so as not to endanger the puppy by putting it in close proximity to other animals which may carry disease.

Specific symptoms apart, the sign that a puppy is not well is often a change in its behaviour; for example, lack of interest in food or in a favourite game or toy, excessive sleepiness, over-excitement or irritability. The owner most likely to detect early signs of trouble is one who knows the puppy well from observation.

Isolated vomiting need be no cause for concern provided there are no other symptoms of illness. A change in diet may well be the reason. An older puppy will often eat grass

Springer Spaniel puppies starting as they hope to go on – with a robust life full of activity. Essentially country dogs, Springers need the stimulation of searching and retrieving.

to induce vomiting if it is feeling uncomfortable.

Some puppies are prone to fits when they are teething. Veterinary advice should be sought at once.

## SIGNS OF HEALTH

**Abdomen**  rounded, not bulging; soft and flexible, not taut or drum-like; not pot-bellied; no swelling around navel.

**Anus**  clean, with no staining, scouring, or matting by dry faeces; it is normal for puppies to sniff under tails to identify other dogs by anal scent.

**Appetite**  enthusiastic for food; no undue scavenging; no vomiting.

**Breathing**  quiet and even when at rest; no laboured breathing; no coughing; normally panting to cool down.

**Claws**  no splitting; no overgrown claws.

**Coat**  clean, pleasant-smelling; free from parasites, loose hairs and dirt; soft to the touch, not staring or brittle.

**Demeanour**  curious, alert, vital; quickly responsive to sounds and calls.

**Ears**  alert to slightest sound; clean, with no brown or yellow deposits; head and ears held in normal position; no scratching, rubbing or shaking of the head.

**Eyes**  clear, with no cloudiness of the cornea; not unduly sensitive to light; no discharge or weeping; not bloodshot.

**Faeces**  consistently formed; colour varying according to diet; should be passed regularly two to four times daily.

**Movement**  tends to be very active in short spurts with rest periods between; young puppies may sleep 16 out of 24 hours; gambolling, unco-ordinated movement normal; young puppies tend to fall over their own feet; no limping or lameness.

**Nose**  condition depends on environment; likely to be cold and damp out of doors, warm and dry indoors; no persistent discharge; nostrils not blocked by dried mucus.

**Pads**  no matting of hair between the digits due to contamination by mud, tar or grease; no cracked pads.

**Skin**  loose and supple; clean, without scurf, inflammation, parasites, or sores.

**Teeth**  clean and white; gums pink except those of the Chow which may show darker pigmentation; shedding of the milk teeth normal (see p.13).

**Urine**  straw-coloured, not cloudy; no blood in the urine; passes urine frequently, with no difficulty; both sexes tend to squat to urinate until puberty, when the male begins to 'cock his leg'.

# *Vaccinations*

Vaccination provides a puppy with protection against certain diseases, so it is important that all puppies should be vaccinated before they start going out for walks, or mixing with other dogs.

The vendor of any puppy should give the new owner written details of any vaccinations. As soon as you get your puppy, ask your veterinary surgeon about completion of the programme and when booster injections will be required.

The record of vaccinations should be kept carefully and produced so that the veterinary surgeon can keep it up to date. No reputable boarding kennels will accept a dog which has not had a full programme of vaccinations.

## INFECTIOUS CANINE DISEASES

Vaccination usually gives protection against seven serious and relatively common diseases (or disease fractions). These are canine distemper (including hardpad), viral hepatitis, parvovirus, two forms of leptospirosis, and both parainfluenza virus and *bordatella bronchiseptica* (each a fraction of the kennel cough complex). Fortunately, it is possible to obtain vaccines which may be used against a combination of diseases simultaneously. Vaccination is very safe and rarely causes an allergic reaction, although the puppy may feel a little drowsy.

## THE VACCINATION REGIME

Most vaccines (but not all) are administered by subcutaneous injection. The usual procedure is for the puppy to receive two injections at an interval of two to four weeks. The first of these is given at between eight and twelve weeks of age, according to the risk factors.

Most young puppies from a reliable source will have received some immunity from their dam, by way of antibodies in her milk. When the first injection has to be given early, the presence of these maternal antibodies can interfere with the effectiveness of the vaccination. Any regime,

The purpose of vaccination is to stimulate the production of the puppy's own antibodies to combat the various disease organisms. This is achieved either by introducing a vaccine of dead disease organisms which cannot produce the disease but will activate the production of antibodies, or by introducing a live vaccine prepared from a weakened strain of the disease (or a strain which attacks other animals) and which is no threat to the puppy. Again, the result will be the production of the puppy's own antibodies.

In countries where rabies is endemic puppies will also need protection against this most dreaded of diseases; indeed vaccination may be mandatory. At present the UK is free of rabies and this is due, almost certainly, to strictly enforced quarantine laws which impose heavy fines on anyone found to have imported *any mammal* without submitting it to a full six months' quarantine at a Ministry-approved kennels.

In the UK vaccination against rabies is available only under permit from the Ministry of Agriculture for animals about to be exported.

therefore, may need adjusting to suit the needs of an individual puppy. For this reason, advice as to the exact timing of the injections should be sought from a veterinary surgeon as soon as the puppy is acquired.

Vaccines do not give life-long protection and all need boosting at regular intervals: some at six months; some after one or two years. Without these booster injections the degree of protection can fall dangerously low.

The puppy's early visits to the veterinary surgeon can help pave the way for a good relationship.

# Ailments and parasites

**Diarrhoea**   This is a very common complaint in puppies. It may be due to the puppy having eaten unfamiliar or unsuitable food, or to an infection caused by bacteria or parasites. It may on rare occasions be due to an obstruction in the intestine as a result of the puppy having swallowed a stone, marble, or other foreign body. If it persists, or is accompanied by vomiting, veterinary advice should be taken. It may be a symptom of disease and produce rapid debilitation through dehydration.

**Worms**   In severe cases, roundworms will be seen in the puppy's faeces, or may be vomited, but even without symptoms, all puppies need to be treated for roundworm infestation. Normally a puppy acquired at eight weeks of age will have been wormed once by the breeder. It is essential, however, that further worming takes place. Do not attempt home cures, but consult your veterinary surgeon when arranging for the puppy's first vaccination.

> Dogs should be wormed about every six months to reduce the risk of passing worm eggs which can lead to serious infection (toxocariasis) in children.

**Ear mites**   A puppy which scratches or rubs its ears, or shakes its head, may have an infestation of ear mites. These parasites feed on the delicate lining of the ear by piercing through the skin. Serum seeps from the wounds to make a characteristic deposit in the ear canal which, in extreme cases, can become completely blocked.

Ear mites can cause intense suffering to a puppy, yet control can be achieved if a prompt veterinary diagnosis is obtained. In neglected cases, the ear drum may be pierced, and permanent middle ear damage can result with such symptoms as loss of balance and convulsions.

**Fleas**   A puppy which scratches itself furiously may be found to have fleas crawling and occasionally jumping through its fur. These reddish-brown parasites feed by piercing the puppy's skin with their mouthparts and sucking on its blood. Flea droppings, which on examination will be seen in the puppy's coat, are in fact the dark colour

Flea

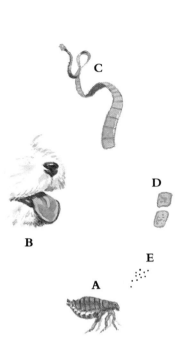

**Life cycle of tapeworm**

**A** Tapeworm develops inside flea.

**B** Flea eaten by dog while grooming.

**C** Adult worm attaches to intestinal wall of dog (can be up to 2 ft long).

**D** Segments of worm break off and are passed in faeces.

**E** Segments break open to release eggs, which are in turn eaten by flea lavae.

of dried blood, containing whole blood cells. There will also be minute clots of blood in the fur, formed when the wounds continue to bleed.

The puncture wounds can become infected, dermatitis may occur, and the flea (as an intermediate host) may transmit tapeworms.

Infestation is most likely in warm weather when the life-cycle of the flea may be as short as 30 days. It is not enough merely to eliminate an infestation from the puppy's coat. Control is only successful when it destroys the fleas in their breeding places, notably the puppy's bed and bedding. Check any other pets for fleas too. Veterinary advice should be taken both on the treatment of the infestation and future prevention. After the fleas have been eradicated, the owner should continue to check for the after-effects mentioned above.

**Lice** An infestation of lice will also make a puppy scratch furiously and frequently. Two species of biting lice and one sucking louse may attack the puppy. The biting lice cannot pierce the skin, but cluster in great numbers around abrasions and at body openings to feed on the natural secretions. Sucking lice pierce the skin to feed. In long-coated puppies it is not easy to see the lice. They are small, dull and rather transparent, and tend to cling to the skin. The white nits – or eggs – however, show up well, particularly on a dark coat.

Puppies suffer great discomfort from lice; the sores caused by scratching may become infected; anaemia may be caused by sucking lice; and biting lice (as intermediate hosts) may transmit tapeworms.

The nits hatch in 7–10 days, and the young are mature at about 14 days. Once fertilized, the female lice lay several eggs a day for their entire life of about 30 days. Veterinary help should be sought if lice are suspected.

**Motion sickness** When travelling by car a high proportion of puppies are affected by motion sickness, with symptoms of nausea, panting and vomiting. The anxiety can also cause diarrhoea. Tranquillizing and anti-motion sickness drugs may be prescribed while the puppy remains prone to such sickness, but most become accustomed to car travel. As soon as the early vaccinations are complete, it helps to take the puppy out in the car twice a day between meal times just for a few minutes at a time.

# Administering medicine

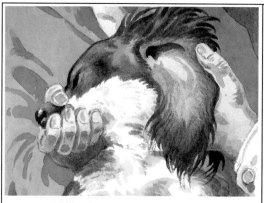

**Holding the muzzle**  It is often necessary to hold a puppy's muzzle while it is being treated. The hand should be closed lightly but firmly over the muzzle, with the thumb on top and the fingers below.

**Tablets**  The top jaw is opened gently with one hand and the lower jaw with the other, leaving thumb and forefinger free to place the tablet well back on the tongue. Then hold the muzzle closed and stroke the throat to assist swallowing.

**Weighing a puppy**  Some puppies are tractable enough to be weighed using kitchen scales. Alternatively, the puppy may be weighed by standing on bathroom scales holding the puppy, and subtracting the handler's weight from the scale reading.

**Holding for examination**
When holding a dog for examination, place one hand round the neck to hold the head steady and the other under the stomach to provide support.

# First aid

The aims of first aid for animals should always be to limit the animal's suffering or injury, keep it as quiet and comfortable as possible, and to seek veterinary help urgently.

## INJURIES
The veterinary surgeon, if contacted by phone and given details of the problem, will advise whether the puppy should be brought to the surgery or should wait to be seen on the spot. Sometimes, as in the case of a road accident, moving the animal may be unavoidable. An injured puppy should be lifted using both arms so that support is distributed evenly. If a fracture is suspected, the puppy should be carried and laid down with the damaged limb uppermost.

## CLEANSING WOUNDS
Pending veterinary attention, major bleeding should be stopped or stemmed by placing a clean handkerchief on the wound. Less major wounds may be bathed in a mild saline solution (1 teaspoon of salt to ½ litre/1 pint of water). Disinfectants or commercial antiseptics should not be used.

## SHOCK
Shock may result from electrocution, wasp or bee stings, burns, poisoning or heart attack. The puppy should be kept warm and if necessary the heart should be massaged gently. Seek veterinary help.

## HEAT EXHAUSTION
Puppies and dogs are prone to heat exhaustion which may result in complete collapse. Puppies that become overheated may be sprinkled with a garden spray or shower attachment to cool them down. They should *not* be plunged into a cold bath as this may be too much of a shock to their systems.

In no circumstances should dogs be left in parked cars, caravans, canvas tents or cabin cruisers.

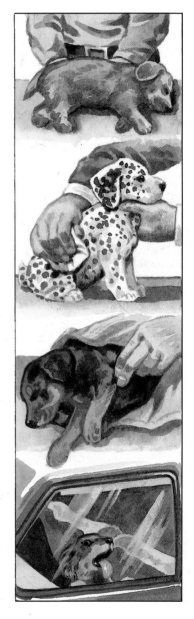

# Dogs and the law

## DOG REGISTRATION

Stray dogs cause many problems in the community – dog fouling, road accidents, and attacks on people and animals. The old licence was abolished in 1988 but the RSPCA believes that a compulsory national registration scheme with the permanent identification of dogs (through silicone chip implant or tattooing, in addition to the existing collar tag) must be introduced to encourage responsible owner-ship. The revenue raised from registration fees would go towards a network of dog wardens who would pick up stray dogs and attempt to reunite them with their owners and administer the law against irresponsible owners.

## DOGS WORRYING LIVESTOCK

The owner or person in charge of a dog found to be worrying livestock is likely to be prosecuted and also to be held liable for heavy damages. In Britain the dog may also be made the subject of a control or destruction order. (Livestock in this case means cattle, sheep, goats, pigs, horses, asses, mules and poultry.) A farmer who shoots a dog in these circumstances is legally in a strong position.

## DANGEROUS DOGS

If a magistrates' court, upon complaint, considers that a dog is dangerous and not properly controlled, even if on the owner's property, it may make an order requiring the owner to control the dog, or alternatively it may order the dog to be destroyed and can appoint a person to carry out the destruction.

In addition, the owner may be disqualified from having custody of a dog for a certain period. Substantial penalities may be imposed for breach of such an order or for failure to hand over a dog for destruction.

## DOGS INVOLVED IN ACCIDENTS

Any driver involved in a road accident with a dog must stop. It is an offence to drive on, knowingly leaving the dog

**Insurance**   The owner of a puppy must expect to have to pay for some routine veterinary treatment and should allow for the cost of this when deciding whether or not to take on the responsibility for a puppy.

In addition it is possible to insure for unexpected veterinary expenses and any legal claim for damages caused by a puppy in, for example, a road accident. Owners are strongly recommended to arrange such insurance, which is available from a number of companies.

For a modest annual premium, a typical policy provides cover for the cost of treatment for accident, injury or illness, with certain exceptions such as vaccinations and neutering. It also covers legal liability, including legal costs, for third party injury or damage to property. Supplementary premiums cover the loss, theft, or accidental death of a pet.

to suffer. The accident must be reported to the police.

The owner of a dog judged to have caused an accident may be liable to third party claims for damage. Readers are advised to buy suitable insurance cover against such a contingency.

## DOG COLLARS

It is compulsory for a dog to wear a collar, bearing the owner's name and address, when in a street or public place. This applies to all pet dogs, although certain others, such as packs of hounds and working sheepdogs, have exemption.

## DOGS AND NUISANCE

Local authorities in the UK have the power to designate certain roads in which dogs must not only wear a collar and identification, but must also be kept on a lead. There may also be bylaws which provide penalties for owners or keepers of dogs which foul public places or which, by repeated barking, cause a nuisance to local residents.

## SUSPECTED CRUELTY CASES

Any reader suspecting that a dog is being subjected to cruelty should ask the RSPCA to investigate the case in confidence. The Inspectors are contacted via the local Group Communciations Centre, which will be listed in the telephone directory under the Royal Society for the Prevention of Cruelty to Animals.

## QUARANTINE REGULATIONS

Strictly enforced UK quarantine laws that require dogs, cats and many other mammals to spend six months in approved quarantine premises on entering the country from abroad have kept Britain virtually free of rabies for over fifty years, although the disease is endemic to most of the world.

Since rabies is now spreading across Europe towards the west, the present fear is that just one pet or stray dog, smuggled in illegally, without the precaution of quarantine, could introduce the disease.

The above is specific to the United Kingdom, but similar laws and regulations are in force in many other countries.

# Your questions answered

**My children think it unfair that if they are given sweets our puppy mustn't have any. Am I right to make this a strict rule?**

Certainly. Sweets damage puppies' teeth at the vital growth stage and can cause obesity and heart conditions later in life. Puppies should not be encouraged to expect 'treats' between meals. Rewards given in training are another matter, but these should be carefully chosen. Many 'dog treats' sold by pet shops contain sugar and are highly unsuitable. Some owners keep a jar of small pieces of wholemeal bread baked hard in the oven and cut into cubes like croûtons. Other suitable rewards include small pieces of charcoal biscuit or, occasionally, fragments of cheese. Remember that rewards lose their value if they are given routinely. They should be given only in recognition of a specific achievement.

**We would like a puppy, but we are all out during the day. Can you recommend a breed that could be left in the house during school and working hours?**

No. No dog should be left on its own all day. Dogs are pack animals, and for the domesticated dog its owner's family takes the place of the pack. To deprive a dog of human company for long periods causes stress and will almost certainly lead to damage to furniture and furnishings as the dog becomes bored. A dog left alone may also create a noise nuisance to neighbours.

**We are planning our holiday. How young can puppies be left in boarding kennels?**

Reputable boarding kennels will not accept puppies that have not completed their initial course of injections, which means an effective minimum of about six months. Always inspect the kennels first. It is a good idea to arrange for a one- or two-night 'induction course' for the puppy's first experience of kennels. This will help it to adjust to a longer stay when you go on holiday.

**My puppy occasionally picks up ticks on walks.
What is the best way to deal with them?**
Do not try to comb or pull the tick out. This will leave its
head still buried in the puppy's skin. Use a drop of surgical
spirit to numb the tick, leave for a few moments until it lets
go, and gently prise it away. An alternative is to coat the
tick with petroleum jelly. This will kill it and it may then be
removed. If, despite these precautions, the head of the tick
remains embedded, veterinary help should be sought.
Anti-tick sprays can be obtained, but in the case of a puppy
under six months check their suitability with a veterinary
surgeon. Anti-tick collars are also available.

**I have seen an advertisement for local obedience
classes. Do you recommend these for my puppy?**
Most owners are able to cope with general obedience
training themselves. The essentials are regular short daily
sessions, with the accent on lavish praise for achievement.
However, if you are a first-time dog owner a class will give
you the basic ground rules and additional confidence. Basic
training (see pp.28-9) is essential, but there is little point in
putting a domestic pet through elaborate routines, which
may give more satisfaction to the owner than to the dog.

**Is it safe to feed my puppy bones?**
A bone gives a puppy great pleasure, and helps the teeth to
form properly. But it *must* be uncooked, large, and without
splintered ends. Never give chop, chicken or game bones.
Rawhide dog-chews from pet shops are a safe and accept-
able alternative.

**When should we buy a collar and tag for our new
puppy?**
There are two reasons for providing a dog with a collar and
identity tag. One is so that it carries a means of identification (and this is a legal requirement in some countries,
including Britain). The other is that, without a collar and
lead any kind of training is virtually impossible. Puppies are
prone to stray and lose their way, and it is recommended
that you fit a light puppy collar from the start. It should be
loose enough for you to be able to slip two fingers easily
between it and the puppy's coat. Giving the puppy a collar
from the beginning avoids possible problems of acceptance
later. You will need to buy a larger collar once or even twice
before the puppy reaches maturity.

# *Life history*

| | |
|---|---|
| Scientific name | *Canis familiaris* |
| Gestation period | 63 days (approx.) |
| Litter size | 1–6 (small breeds)<br>5–12 (large breeds) |
| Birth weight | 100 g/3½ oz–<br>500 g/1 lb 2 oz |
| Eyes open | 10 days |
| Weaning age | 35-49 days |
| Weaning weight | 1 kg/2 lb 4 oz<br>(small breeds) |
| Puberty | males 8–12 months<br>females 6–18 months<br>(commonly 8 months) |
| Adult weight | 1 kg/2 lb 4 oz–<br>70 kg/150 lb |
| Best age to breed | males 350+ days<br>females 540+ days |
| Oestrus (or season) | 2 seasons per year |
| Duration of oestrus | 3 weeks |
| Retire from breeding | males 8 years<br>females 6–8 years |
| Life expectancy | 10–18 years (small dogs<br>usually outlive larger<br>breeds) |

# *Record card*

Record sheet for your own puppy

(photograph or portrait)

Name

Date of birth
(actual or estimated)

Breed                          Sex

Colour/description

Feeding notes

Medical record                          Date of first season

Date of neutering operation

Veterinary treatment:   dates:

Worming

Vaccinations

Veterinary surgeon's name                          Surgery hours

Practice address

Tel. no.

# Index